Original title:
Life: A Series of Mistakes and Laughs

Copyright © 2025 Creative Arts Management OÜ
All rights reserved.

Author: Adrian Caldwell
ISBN HARDBACK: 978-1-80566-116-0
ISBN PAPERBACK: 978-1-80566-411-6

Lighthearted Lessons

In the grand parade of blunders,
We trip and giggle, what a sight!
Falling face-first into blunders,
Oh, the way we laugh in flight!

Each misstep's a tickled treasure,
A dance of folly on the stage.
We learn with each silly measure,
Embrace the fun, let joy engage!

The Happy Accidents

A coffee spill upon the floor,
Turns into laughter, what a play!
With every slip, we laugh some more,
Who knew mistakes could save the day?

The cake that crumbled, oh so sweet,
A frosted mess, our fondest treat.
In every error, giggles greet,
As happiness finds its quick retreat!

Amusements in Anomalies

In a world of quirky ways,
We stumble on through day and night.
Taking detours, finding rays,
Of laughter chasing wrongs so bright!

Missed the bus but met a friend,
Turned an error into cheer.
With every twist, there's joy to send,
Life's sweetest laughs draw ever near!

Cartwheels of Chance

With hands in pockets, we just slip,
Into the joy of happy hints.
Cartwheels of fate, we bravely flip,
As clumsy fate brings forth its prints.

From silly falls to silly cheers,
We dance through mishaps, hearts aglow.
In laughter's echo, drop our fears,
For it's the fun that helps us grow!

The Playful Paradox

I tripped on my own two feet,
A dance gone wildly wrong,
Laughter erupted like a cheer,
Mistakes seem to keep me strong.

With each slip, a story grows,
Life's little jokes unfold,
Bumps and bruises tell me so,
Adventures never get old.

Silliness Amidst Snares

I wore my shirt inside out,
A fashion statement bold,
Friends burst into hearty shouts,
My style they deemed pure gold.

Stuck in a closet? What a sight!
I laughed at my own plight,
Puzzles in the wrong place,
Silliness, oh what a grace!

Revelry in the Ruins

A cupcake dropped, icing smeared,
Frosting on my nose a thrill,
Everyone around just cheered,
In chaos, laughter can fulfill.

Stumbling through a crowded space,
I turned to find my lost shoe,
Each mishap a joyful race,
In mess, I find my view.

Wandering through Whimsy

I chased a butterfly, oh dear,
Fell flat upon the ground,
Laughter echoed far and near,
Joy in the stumble found.

Life's a circus with no tent,
Clowns and giggles in the air,
Every mistake, a precious gem,
Silly moments we all share.

Grins Through the Gaffes

In a dance of missteps, we twirl and spin,
Our laughter erupts, where blunders begin.
With a wink and a grin, we fumble our way,
Every slip on the floor turns night into day.

A spaghetti mishap, it lands on my shoe,
But who needs a plate? I've got the best view!
We toast to our chaos with cups held on high,
For each silly moment, like stars in the sky.

With hiccups and giggles, our secrets unfold,
A wardrobe malfunction, two shirts made of gold.
Like clowns in a circus, we weave through our day,
Collecting the laughs, come what may.

In the end, as we chalk up the blunders so grand,
We celebrate joys that slip through our hands.
For every misadventure we've shared through the years,
We gather our stories, tempered with cheers.

Trifles and Triumphs

A trip on a sidewalk, down I go thud,
But up comes a chuckle, from out of the mud.
With coffee in hand, I spill on my clothes,
I wear all my blunders like lovely bright bows.

Each little mistake turns into a treat,
Jugging my ego, I dance on my feet.
The cat steals my lunch, he's a clever old chap,
With crumbs on my shirt, I laugh at the snap.

A flat tire sends us on trails far and wide,
Each wrong turn we make, I won't run and hide.
We pop the champagne for the pitfalls we face,
Finding joy in the stumbles, that's our saving grace.

As the sun starts to set on the goofs we've embraced,
We gather the moments, in joy interlaced.
For every odd twist of this whimsical path,
We'll dance through mistakes, wrapped up in our laugh.

Tragicomedy of Mistakes

Once I tripped on my own shoe,
A stumble that no one knew,
Laughter bubbled like a spring,
Oh, the joy that slips can bring.

In the kitchen, I tossed some peas,
They flew like birds, oh such a tease,
Dinner turned into a game of catch,
My guests laughed, saying, "What a match!"

A phone call made to say 'hello',
Ended up as a rhythmic show,
Forgot my words, just made a rhyme,
Who knew blunders could sound so fine?

Every mishap, a chance to cheer,
With giggles shared from ear to ear,
In the play of folly, let us bask,
For humor's the answer to every task.

Smirks from Miscalculations

I once thought I could bake a cake,
Flour exploded, what a mistake,
My kitchen looked like snowy bliss,
Who knew chaos could taste like this?

Driving down the road, I turned wrong,
Found a cafe that felt like a song,
With every twist, I learned to dance,
A misstep sometimes leads to chance.

I borrowed clothes, a fashion thrill,
Ended up looking like a pill,
Yet in the mirror, I couldn't frown,
I wore my blunders like a crown.

In every goof, we find a clue,
That laughter's magic shines right through,
So here's to fun when plans go south,
With smiles and giggles we'll laugh it out.

The Mirthful Misadventures

My pet parrot learned to talk,
But all it said was, "Take a walk!"
As I tried to teach it grace,
It squawked out loud in public space.

In yoga class, I lost my way,
Found my balance in disarray,
Fell and landed near a cat,
Even felines know where it's at.

I signed up for a dance off, bold,
But my two left feet just got cold,
Spinning round brought cheers and giggles,
And all my foes just teased with wiggles.

Each blunder made a merry tale,
In mischief's grip, we shall not fail,
With laughter's song, let's all embrace,
The joys of life's most silly space.

Winks at Wardrobe Malfunctions

My zipper caught in a sudden race,
Left my dignity in quite a place,
The crowd just chuckled as I blushed,
A symbol of fashion, now crushed.

Tights that ripped mid-dance floor cheer,
Led to laughter, loud and clear,
With every twist, my woes did sway,
Who knew a tear could make my day?

A shirt that shrank in the warm wash,
Now fit my doll, oh what a posh,
I strutted out with panache so bright,
Charmed the room with humor's light.

So here's to mishaps, let's all cheer,
In quirky moments, we shed a tear,
With winks and giggles, life shines through,
For laughter's fabric fits us too.

The Humor of the Human Experience

We stumble through the daily grind,
With quirky thoughts that cross our mind.
A misstep here, a slip of grace,
We find the joy in our own race.

The coffee spills, a shirt's askew,
Yet laughter bubbles, fresh and new.
With each mistake, a lesson learned,
In craziness, our hearts have turned.

We juggle dreams, we trip and fall,
Embrace the chaos, give it all.
The humor shines in blunders made,
We dance through life, together swayed.

With every fumble, giggles rise,
We share our tales, and every sigh.
The joy of living, just a jest,
In foolish moments, we find rest.

Chuckles Wrapped in Confusion

In tangled thoughts, we search for sense,
While faces twist and minds commence.
A glance misread, a wrong wrap-up,
Confusion brews, we raise a cup.

What's that you said? A twisty phrase!
In every mix-up, laughter stays.
We trip on words, then spin around,
In silly knots, our joy is found.

A wardrobe choice gone so awry,
With mismatched socks, we waltz on by.
The blunders thick, like syrup flow,
We're wrapped in giggles, through the show.

So here's to those perplexing days,
When things don't go the usual ways.
With humor as our trusty guide,
In every mess, we take great pride.

The Adventure of the Awkward

We set out brave, a step or three,
Then trip on air, how can this be?
With every fumble, smiles ignite,
Our awkwardness becomes delight.

A wave gone wrong, a missed high-five,
In bumbling form, we feel alive.
With every laugh, we draw near close,
In comedy of errors, we boast.

Like penguins sliding on the floor,
We wobble, laugh, and ask for more.
Each cringe a story, bold and bright,
We weave our tales into the night.

So raise a glass to moments clumsy,
To every crack where we grow fumbly.
In awkward steps, our truth we see,
The thrill of fun for you and me.

Unforeseen Excursions

We mapped it out, or so we thought,
But paths diverge, our plans are caught.
In deviations, wonders bloom,
We chase the fun, forget the gloom.

A wrong turn leads to gelato stands,
With toppings tossed by careless hands.
Explorers bold in curiosity,
In misadventures, we find glee.

Flip-flops on and hats askew,
We dance in rain, with skies so blue.
Unplanned stops make dinner grand,
Together munching, hand in hand.

In every twist, a joy awaits,
Our hearts embrace what fortune states.
For in the mess of unexpected,
We find a path, forever connected.

Rascals of Randomness

In a world of slips and trips,
We tumble, we laugh, we do some flips.
Each blunder a badge we wear with pride,
As we dance through the chaos, side by side.

With every misstep, a giggle bursts,
As we quench our failures with joyful thirsts.
For in every fall, there's joy to find,
The rascals of randomness, humor combined.

A pie in the face, a shoe on the wrong,
All these mishaps, they help us belong.
So let's raise a toast to our silly ways,
Cultivating laughter through all our days.

Glitches and Giggles

In a glitchy world where laughter thrives,
Each mishap sings as spontaneity derives.
With laughter that bubbles, spills like a brook,
We're the jokers, the jesters, life's comic book.

Oops, there went my cereal on the floor,
A splash of milk and I'm out the door.
Laughter erupts with each silly slip,
These moments of joy are the best road trip.

We stitch our days with giggles so bright,
Finding humor in chaos, that feels just right.
So here's to the mischief our hearts always seek,
In glitches and giggles, we find our peak.

Frayed Edges of Wisdom

With frayed edges and a tattered tie,
We stumble through wisdom, oh my, oh my.
Every lesson learned with a comical twist,
In the book of our blunders, nothing is missed.

A slip of the tongue, a strange outfit choice,
In moments of awkward, we laugh and rejoice.
For each crack of wisdom, life gives us flair,
With a chuckle that dances in the crisp air.

So here's to the frayed, the patched, the torn,
In our mosaic of blunders, we are reborn.
Finding clarity wrapped in a riddle,
We laugh through the chaos, it is the middle.

The Chronicles of Chipper Chaos

In the chronicles of our chipper spree,
We paint our blunders like a gallery.
With colors of laughter and brushstrokes of glee,
Each fumble is art, just wait and see.

With a hop and a skip, we tumble and sway,
Our stories are woven in a playful display.
Every twist and turn, a new little jest,
In this raucous tale, we're truly blessed.

The hiccup of fate, the blender gone wild,
Our laughter is nursey, just like a child.
So gather around, let the chaos unfold,
These chronicles cherished, bright memories told.

Whimsy in the Wrong Turns

I took a left when I should've gone right,
And stumbled into a clown's delight.
With pies in the face and laughter so loud,
I found my mistake was the best kind of crowd.

The roads were twisted, my map was a joke,
Every detour, a whimsical poke.
I waved at a duck, who winked with a grin,
In this wacky adventure, how could I not win?

From sidewalks to puddles, I danced in the rain,
Each splatter and slip made me forget my pain.
With friends made of giggles and silly charm,
My wrong turns always kept me warm.

So here's to the blunders, the fumbles in style,
Life's chaotic moments make the journey worthwhile.
For in every wrong turn, there's magic to find,
A treasure of laughter, smiling unconfined.

Tumbles and Triumphs

I tripped on my shoelace, fell flat on my face,
Yet burst into laughter, what a funny place!
My tumble brought joy to the folks passing by,
    A slip of the foot turned into a high five.

The coffee I spilled, an artistic display,
Swirls of brown chaos brightened my day.
As I wiped at the mess, I couldn't help but cheer,
Who knew a mishap could spread so much cheer?

Running through life with a hop and a skip,
Each wobble and wobble, a delightful trip.
For every small stumble that leads me astray,
    A triumph emerges in a silly ballet.

With friends gathered round, sharing tales of the fun,
Mistakes blend in laughter, my heart weighs a ton.
For it's not just the wins, but the falls that ignite,
    A joyous reminder that wrong can feel right.

Joyful Misdirections

I asked for directions but got lost in a grin,
The map was a riddle, where do I begin?
With every wrong alley, I found something neat,
A taco truck dancing to a funky beat.

I wandered in circles, but found a cute cat,
Who zipped through a fence, oh where's that at?
With a chase and a laugh, I fell down in bliss,
Sometimes the wrong path brings pure happiness.

I tried to impress with a fancy new move,
But ended in giggles, lost all sense of groove.
Jumps turned to flails, my style less than cool,
Yet everyone laughed, and I played the fool.

So here's to missteps that lighten the load,
To joyful detours on this wild road.
For every small blunder is a story to tell,
Wrapped in warm laughter, we all know it well.

The Dance of Error

I began to tango, but forgot all the steps,
With two left feet, I looked like a pest.
My partner spun fast, while I spun in place,
A twirl and a trip became part of the grace.

Mistakes took the lead, and I followed along,
Each clap was a hiccup, but still, we were strong.
We laughed and we fumbled, like stars in a show,
In this waltz of error, we danced with the flow.

When plans went awry, we just went with the breeze,
Exploring the oddities, with giggles that tease.
A jester of joy in every blundered turn,
Reminds us it's okay, it's how we all learn.

So let's keep on dancing, embrace every fall,
For the best kind of moments are the ones we recall.
In the rhythm of laughter, the stumbles are sweet,
In the dance of our errors, our joy is complete.

Lessons Wrapped in Laughter

Fell off my chair, what a sight,
Laughter erupted, pure delight.
I tripped on a shoe, made a fall,
Yet here we are, laughing through it all.

A cake I baked, it quite flopped,
With frosting too thick, I just stopped.
We shared a slice, and we grinned,
In every fail, a fun story pinned.

Chasing a cat, what a chase,
Ended up with cream on my face.
With each blunder, joy takes flight,
In every mishap, we find our light.

So let's toast to blunders, my friends,
The laughter lingers and never ends.
In messy moments, we see the grace,
Each giggle a blessing, sweet embrace.

The Dance of Imperfections

Two left feet on the dance floor,
Stepped on my friend, awkward galore!
We spun and twirled, fell to the ground,
In goofy rhythm, our joy was found.

Forgot my lines, stuttered and paused,
The crowd erupted; how great we caused!
With every fumble, a story to tell,
Each step a misstep, but oh so well.

In messy hair and mismatched socks,
We giggle through all the paradox.
A dance of quirks, in sync we sway,
In every flaw, we find our play.

Let's embrace the wobbles in our stride,
With every laugh, we take it in pride.
In this wild dance, let's not conform,
For joy is found in the abnormal.

Hiccups and Hilarity

A sneeze, a cough, the hiccup spree,
Laughing with friends, what a jubilee!
We spill our drinks, what a mess!
Still, we giggle, nothing less.

A wrong text sent, oh what a blunder,
A mix-up that left us laughing asunder.
In every awkward, comical slip,
We sip our jokes, take another dip.

The cat leaped high, knocked down my lunch,
Tomato flew like a punch!
Rolling with laughter, we let it slide,
In every laugh, joy is our guide.

So here's to the quirks that make us whole,
Celebrating gaffes, that's our goal.
With each little hiccup, we raise a cheer,
In the chaos of humor, we find our sphere.

Serendipitous Snafus

Woke up late, missed the bus ride,
Chased it down, tripped on the side.
With coffee spill and a race against time,
Yet laughter echoed, everything rhymed.

A birthday surprise, gift wrapped awry,
The cat hid inside, oh my, oh my!
The candles blew out, one too soon,
Still, we guffawed under the moon.

In juggling tasks, I dropped a few,
Potato chips flew, as they often do!
Ripped my pants, a fashion faux pas,
Yet with every laugh, life feels bizarre.

So here's to the blunders, let's celebrate,
In these slapstick moments, we elevate.
For every snafu brings peals of joy,
In the humor of mishaps, we find our ploy.

The Dance of Delightful Disarray

In a twist of fate, I tripped and fell,
Laughter erupted, like a ringing bell.
With shoes on the wrong feet, I danced a jig,
My friends laughed hard, oh what a gig!

Spilled my drink, a colorful splash,
I wore my folly like a vibrant sash.
With each clumsy step, a grin appeared,
Oops, I did it again, but never feared!

Chasing the cat, I tumbled down,
Rolling like a jester in this silly town.
Even the lamp gave a hearty cheer,
For every faux pas brought friends near!

So let the music play and hearts collide,
In this grand ballet, where joys abide.
With every twist, we turn delight,
Cheering for blunders in laughter's light.

Snicker in the Shadows

Whispers of blunders lurk in the night,
A forgotten key, and I lost my flight.
Under the streetlight, I gave a shout,
As my sandwich flew; oh, what a bout!

Stumbling upon secrets, I tried to be sly,
But tripped on my shoelace while giving a try.
The moon paused a moment, chuckled a bit,
Watching my antics, I just wouldn't quit!

A knock at the door, it was the wrong place,
I greeted the mailman with a curious face.
We laughed as I blurted my birthday surprise,
Not even his frown could hide the clever eyes!

With every mishap, a giggle grew loud,
In the shadows of oops, I felt quite proud.
For it's in the goofs we often find cheer,
Embracing the folly that keeps us all near.

The Cheer in the Chaotic

Chaos erupted, much to my delight,
A cat in the kitchen gave quite a fright.
Flour in the air, I sneezed with a grin,
The cookies were ruined, but laughter crept in.

Dancing around with a mop in my hand,
I slipped on a puddle, it went as I planned.
With squeals and giggles, the mess turned to fun,
Pandemonium's charm came out one by one.

Painting the wall, oh what a sight,
I smeared more on me than the canvas so bright.
With colors that clashed, I wore my new art,
The laughter erupted, a masterpiece of heart.

Even in shambles, a joy we create,
Unruly moments that never abate.
Through chaos and blunders, we're never alone,
In the cheer of mayhem, our hearts have grown!

Hilarity in Hiccups

A hiccup escaped at the most wrong time,
While sipping my tea, it turned to a rhyme.
Each little spasm, a musical score,
Sipped some more soda—oh, there's one more!

At the big dinner, my hiccups burst forth,
My uncle just laughed, as I'd just lost worth.
With every disruption, we giggled and sipped,
Hiccups a signal, our humor we flipped.

Trying to sing, oh what a mistake,
Each note accompanied by a hiccup quake.
Yet there in the giggles, and laughter's embrace,
We found joy together, in this funny space.

So rather than fret when you make a sound,
Embrace the absurdness that's all around.
For in every hiccup, a story resides,
Where laughter's the bridge, and joy surely bides.

The Art of Falling Gracefully

Tripped on my shoelace, quite the display,
Laughter erupted, brightened the day.
Ground's got a charm, it welcomes the fall,
With every tumble, I stand up tall.

Each misstep's a dance, a clumsy ballet,
Falling, I find joy in this wayward sway.
Giggles erupt as my dignity fades,
Embracing the flaws the universe laid.

Like a cartoon who slips on a pie,
I wiggle and wobble, oh me, oh my!
For every mishap, there's humor, it shows,
In each little glance, as the silly wind blows.

So here's to the faceplants, the blunders ahead,
I'll cherish the laughter, not worry instead.
With every wrong turn, there's a story to share,
In the art of the fall, there's magic somewhere.

Lessons from the Left Turn

Took a left when I meant to go right,
Ended up giggling at the bizarre sight.
A detour led me to a clown's parade,
Life's funny twists, like a well-timed charade.

Navigating chaos, my map's gone askew,
But every wrong road brings a thrill brand new.
Waving at strangers, feeling quite grand,
Adventures await when you don't have a plan.

A shortcut to joy in the misread of fate,
Stumbling on magic that isn't too late.
Flip-flops and flubs make the best kind of tales,
With laughter and joy, the heart never fails.

So when you find trouble, in the most silly ways,
Know that the left turn can brighten your days.
In the dance of confusion, there's light in the fray,
Just laugh and embrace it, come what may.

Mischief in the Mundane

A spilled cup of coffee, a chore gone awry,
In mundane moments, see how we fly.
A splash and a chuckle, a playful delight,
Finding mischief in the day's simple plight.

Dust bunnies whirl like a dance in the air,
The vacuum sings songs of misguided flair.
Turning chores into games, oh what a thrill,
With laughter galore, daily grind becomes chill.

Laundry's a puzzle, a magical maze,
Socks play hide and seek, adding to the craze.
Such hilarity dwells in the ordinary scene,
In life's little moments, we reign as the queen.

So let's cheer for the blunders, the fun in the grind,
For mischief makes memories, of the joyful kind.
Embrace the slip-ups, the chaos, the cheer,
In the mundane, sweet laughter is always near.

Giggles Between the Cracks

In tiny nooks where the giggles reside,
Laughter escapes, no need to hide.
Cracks in the pavement, with stories they've told,
Dance of the absurd, let the play unfold.

Fallen leaves whisper secrets of old,
In every mishap, find wonders untold.
Banana peels waiting, just watch where you tread,
Life's little hiccups, a fountain of red.

Under the table, the cat gets her bath,
While I slip on marbles and fall with a laugh.
Shadows of blunders, they toss and they turn,
In the cracks, pure joy, like candles they burn.

So let's seek the giggles, the joy in surprise,
In each little error, true humor lies.
For amidst all the chaos, it's clear to perceive,
In the laughter we share, we truly believe.

Mirth Among the Mishaps

Tripped on my shoelace today,
Landed in a flower bed,
Bees thought I was their friend,
Now I wear a buzz instead.

Coffee spilled right on my shirt,
Guess I'm the fashion trend,
Style is all about the spill,
Cheers to clumsy lives we blend.

Fell off the chair in the meeting,
Laughter echoed, oh so bright,
Who knew a tumble like that,
Would lead to our best insight?

Each blunder adds a new tale,
We shrug, we laugh, we sing,
In the mess, we find our grace,
It's joy that makes us swing.

What Ifs and Whoopsies

What if I try cooking tonight?
Oh no! That smoke alarm's a fright,
Dinner's now a crispy mess,
But laughing feels like pure success.

What if my shoes are mismatched?
Strangers smile, I'm quite attached,
Colors clash like art on walls,
Who knew joy could break the falls?

What if this dance is too wild?
I twirl and spin, feel like a child,
Echoes of giggles fill the air,
Our blunders make us quite the pair.

What if we let worries slide?
Embrace the chaos, take a ride,
Each slip becomes a cherished tale,
We find our way, we will not fail.

Ripple of Resilience

A wave of laughter strikes the shore,
From silly slips that we adore,
We fall and get back on our feet,
With every blunder, life's a treat.

Like juggling eggs, I made a mess,
One slipped and caused a great distress,
Yet from the yolk, a smile emerged,
In that moment, joy surged.

A paintbrush slipped, the canvas smeared,
The art I sought, yet I persevered,
Now colors blend in ways unknown,
Each splatter tells the tale I own.

Look at the world through laughter's lens,
Every fumble only lightens bends,
Together we'll weave a tapestry,
Of silliness and sweet jubilee.

Doodles of Delightful Mistakes

With crayons in hand, I make a dash,
A sun looks like an orange smash,
But my masterpiece brings joy anew,
Who knew mistakes made colors bloom?

I wrote the wrong name on a cake,
It read 'Happy Birth', for goodness' sake,
We laughed and sang 'Birthday to You',
The best moments arise from what's askew.

A puppy chewed my homework thin,
The answer was 'woof', a silly win,
Yet in the chaos, a lesson spoke,
Laughter and love, that is the joke.

So let's doodle and play with glee,
Embrace what is wild and carefree,
In every mix-up, we find our light,
As we dance through the day and night.

Joy in the Missteps

I tripped on a shoelace, oh what a sight,
Laughter erupted, a pure delight.
I danced with my coffee, spilled on my shoes,
And all of my worries, I happily lose.

Chasing my cat, I thought I could fly,
But landed in bushes, oh me, oh my!
With every odd tumble, there's giggles in store,
Embracing the chaos, who could ask for more?

I slipped on a rug, did a flawless twirl,
Turns out that my clumsiness is quite the pearl.
Each misstep a treasure, a chuckle's embrace,
Finding joy in the moments that life can't erase.

So here's to the blunders, the laughs that we share,
In the midst of the chaos, we find our flare.
With a wink and a grin, let's gather and play,
For joy blooms in blunders, come what may.

The Symphony of Errors

A concerto of chaos, my socks don't quite match,
Each note of my life, a comedic scratch.
I fumbled through breakfast, spilled milk on my shirt,
Yet laughter composed, as I slipped in the dirt.

The cat stole my toast, with a meow so refined,
While I chased the toast thief, I laughed and felt blind.
In my juggling of tasks, I forgot one or two,
But who needs perfection when giggles ensue?

Each day is a canvas, of blunders and cheer,
With a drumroll of missteps, the rhythm's sincere.
So grab a front-row seat, watch this show unfold,
In the symphony of errors, brave tales will be told.

A wink at the world, as I trip on my way,
The sweet sound of laughter will surely stay.
With grace in our falls, and joy in our hum,
Life is a comedy, oh how we succumb!

Chuckles in Chaos

A sprightly little dance, I fell on my face,
Laughter erupted, it's a wild embrace.
Chasing my dreams, I run into a wall,
But oh, how I giggle, I'm having a ball!

A blender explosion, what a messy blast,
Smoothie splatters everywhere, memories cast.
I wore a bright grin while the kitchen was wet,
In this grand comedy, no chance for regret.

My pants told a tale, a rip with a breeze,
As I bowed to my friends, I was brought to my knees.
With jokes in the air and mishaps on cue,
We revel in chaos, it's what we all do.

So here's to the laughter, the folly we share,
With chuckles and quirks woven deep in the air.
Through every small blunder, we find our delight,
In this topsy-turvy world that feels just right.

Whimsical Follies

In my quest for the perfect, I wobble and sway,
Each step is a jest, and I laugh all the way.
I topple through puddles, splash beautiful art,
The magic of mishaps, they steal every heart.

With mismatched shoes, I prance through the park,
Each glance I receive adds to our lark.
A giggle here, a trip over there,
In the whimsical follies, there's joy everywhere.

A dance with my dog, we both lose the beat,
As we tumble together, we can't find our feet.
But laughter, oh laughter, it bubbles and gleams,
Like confetti in chaos, fulfilling our dreams.

So let's raise a glass to the fumbles we make,
Each folly a treasure, no heart ever aches.
In every odd moment, a story will bloom,
In the garden of giggles, we vanish the gloom.

Chronicles of a Comical Fumble

I tripped on my shoelace, oh what a sight,
With arms in the air, I took flight.
A pigeon laughed hard, a scene so grand,
And I landed with grace, not quite what I planned.

I tried to impress with a dance move slick,
But ended up spinning, felt like a brick.
The cat looked amused, with eyes so wide,
As I toppled again, I had nowhere to hide.

Breakfast was chaos, the toast took a dive,
Butter went flying, oh how I thrived!
With laughter erupting from all in the room,
I wiped my hands clean, I spread joy, not gloom.

So here's to the blunders, the slips and the falls,
Each giggle and chuckle, the best of us all.
In the carnival of life, we twirl with delight,
Making memories that sparkle, so brilliantly bright.

The Joy of Missteps

I wore mismatched socks, a fashion faux pas,
But strangers just chuckled, and said, 'Hurrah!'
An umbrella opened, a gusty surprise,
The laugh of a child lit up the skies.

I thought I was clever, with jokes on my tongue,
But stumbles on punchlines left everyone sprung.
With groans and with giggles, we shared the delight,
As I fumbled my way to the end of the night.

I carved out a pumpkin for Halloween cheer,
But it ended up looking like something from fear.
The neighbors just howled, what a terrible sight,
Yet laughter erupted, our hearts felt so light.

So raise a toast high to each silly fall,
To the moments we cherish, we'll treasure them all.
For in all our blunders, there's joy to be found,
In the dance of the foolish, we're merrily bound.

Forgotten Follies

I cooked up a feast, it was meant to impress,
But it turned into chaos, oh what a mess!
The chicken was dancing, the veggies took flight,
And we roasted our laughter till late in the night.

I tried to be swift on an ice-skating date,
But gravity chuckled, oh why tempt fate?
Spinning and twirling, I secured my fame,
As I landed in snow, they all cheered my name!

A surprise birthday bash went awry with a bang,
The balloons were all tied, then suddenly sprang.
Floating away, like wishes gone wild,
We chased them with laughter, just like a child.

So here's to the times we forget and we fumble,
To the giggles that rise when we trip and we stumble.
In this wacky jungle, the heart finds its way,
For every mishap, there's joy when we play.

Serenade of Silly Stumbles

With a wig on my head, I danced through the square,
A gust of the wind sent it up in the air.
The crowd roared with laughter, I took a bow,
As I grinned in the chaos, just living in the now.

I set out to jog, my sneakers untied,
A tumble and roll left my dignity fried.
But the dog that passed by joined in my fall,
Together we tumbled, what fun to recall!

I attempted to sing, hit a note way too high,
A blend of a cat and a startled goodbye.
The chorus erupted in giggles and cheer,
As I found my missteps brought more people near.

So laugh with abandon, embrace every slip,
For the sweetest of moments come not from the script.
With each silly stumble, we dance and we play,
In the hilarity, the heart finds its way.

Chucking in the Shadows

When I tried to dance like a pro,
My feet had a mind of their own.
I tripped on a cat and landed with grace,
Now the dog mocks my moves, what a place!

Coffee on my shirt, oh what a sight,
I swear it was black, not a caramel fright.
Cheers to the spills that brought on a grin,
Even my coffee knows how to win!

I thought I'd bake cookies, a sweet little treat,
But flour erupted like a white street.
With powdered sugar clouds, I declared my defeat,
Yet laughter filled the air, oh what a feat!

So here's to the blunders and giggles we share,
For in every mishap, there's joy to declare.
In shadows we chuckle, embracing each fall,
It's the humor in moments that triumphs in all!

The Jester's Journey

With a hat full of bells, I set out to play,
But my shoes had other plans, led me astray.
I juggled my worries, oh what a sight,
Each flop and each drop turned wrongs into right.

The audience laughed as I slipped on a pie,
A clown's best friend, oh me, oh my!
With a honk and a tumble, I bloomed like a flower,
Mistakes on my stage gave humor great power.

My path twisted wild like a winding old route,
With each silly stumble, I found a new route.
A pratfall in rain, I danced in a puddle,
A splash and a giggle, an escape from the muddle.

So I'll wear my bright nose through thick and through thin,
For every faux pas invites the joy in.
The jester's journey is best if we dare,
To laugh at the slips and show that we care!

Waltzing with Blunders

I stepped on my toes in a grand old waltz,
The mirror cracked up as I spinned and revolved.
With missteps aplenty, I jumped and I swayed,
Yet the laughs that erupted left worries delayed.

A banana peel dance became quite the show,
As friends hit the floor, I stole the front row.
Oops! Oh so graceful, we all hit a wall,
But laughter rang louder, we had a ball!

In a kitchen disaster, I mixed up my spoons,
Potato chip soup? Come dine with the goons!
Each bite was an adventure, a flavorful mess,
But cheers filled the table, in laughter we're blessed.

So raise up a glass to the ups and the downs,
To the clutter and chaos, the goldmine of clowns.
For waltzing with blunders, a dance so divine,
Is where joy meets the missteps with a wink and a smile!

Echoes of Laughter

In the park with my kite, took off like a dream,
But the wind had a plan, or so it would seem.
Up in the tree, my joy went astray,
Yet echoes of laughter turned night into day.

I wore mismatched socks on a casual spree,
"Fashion statement!" I claimed as they laughed at me.
Each quirk in the mirror, a tickle or two,
Life's best little jokes are found in the stew.

When cooking is chaos and dinner's a flop,
A flame-wreathed pancake? Just call it a prop!
With forks turned to spoons and giggles sincere,
We toast to blunders and toasting with cheer.

So gather the moments we treasure and keep,
In echoes of laughter, our worries fall steep.
For the joy that mistakes bring along with sweet grins,
Are the tales that we share where the fun truly begins!

The Comedic Compass

In a world of goofy turns,
We trip on laughter's way.
With each misstep, brightly burns,
A smile to greet the day.

Maps drawn with crayon, oh so bold,
Lead us far off track.
Yet in tales of stumbles told,
We find the fun we lack.

Puns drop like breadcrumbs in the park,
Wandering paths with glee.
A joke that lands—oh, such a spark!
We giggle endlessly.

With every twist and silly bump,
We dance without a care.
In the chaos, join the jump,
And laugh without a stare.

Flawed Yet Funny

Mistakes parade in vibrant hues,
Each blunder's like a show.
In every fumble, we choose,
To laugh instead of slow.

With socks that clash and mismatched shoes,
We sculpt our comedy.
In chaos, happiness we lose,
Yet find odd harmony.

The mirror's grin, a friend so true,
Reflects our every fall.
With every slip, we dance anew,
Oh, what a joyful call!

So let us wear the silly crown,
And cheer for every slip.
Embrace this twisted merry town,
And take a funny trip.

Wanderings of Witty Miscalculations

I took a turn that wasn't planned,
Right into a pie!
With berries flying through the air,
My luck, oh me, oh my!

Each detour brings a spark of fun,
As laughter fills the void.
Through clumsy acts, our hearts are won,
With joy that's unalloyed.

A recipe that flops and flips,
A cake that leans and bends.
We taste our failures, laugh, and dip,
In friendship that transcends.

So let's embrace our quirky ways,
And share a chuckling glance.
In silly moments, bright displays,
We find our sweetest dance.

Joy in the Juxtaposition

In life's grand play, we often fail,
With humor stitched in seams.
Each mishap spins a comic tale,
And fuels our wildest dreams.

The cat that jumps and lands askew,
The cake that's burnt and flat.
In every stumble, something new,
We giggle at the spat.

With witty lines and goofy stares,
We weave our happy song.
In every flaw, a laughter bares,
To dance where we belong.

So twirl around in playful glee,
Embrace each wild mistake.
For joy is found in mischief's spree,
A funny path we make.

Chronicles of Curious Choices

In the kitchen I tried, to bake a fine pie,
But the flour flew high, like birds in the sky.
The sugar I mistook, for a salt shaker prank,
Now the guests all say, it's a taste they can't rank.

I wore mismatched socks, just to feel free,
One spotted, one striped, a bold fashion spree.
But then on the street, a kid pointed and laughed,
Guess my sense of style has gone quite daft!

I sent a sweet text to my boss, oh dear,
Meant for my friend, who loves cheese and beer.
He replied with a grin, "I'm not that inspired,"
Now our office talks revolve 'round what's required.

So here's to the blunders, the giggles they bring,
The dances we stumble, or accidentally sing.
With every odd turn that forges our path,
We find joy in the chaos, and chuckles in wrath.

The Symphony of Slips

A slip of the tongue, it landed with flair,
I complimented the cat, called it a bear.
The owner just chuckled, "Why sit and explain?"
Now every feline wears a teddy's domain.

I tripped on the stairs, a graceful cascade,
Like a clown on a mission, the effect was well played.
The neighbor just cheered, "Bravo, take a bow!"
With antics like this, I'm the star of the show.

My phone's autocorrect, a mischievous sprite,
Changed 'meet at six' to 'let's eat tonight!'
Now dinner's a party, where spaghetti takes flight,
My new friends are pasta, they twirl with delight.

So raise a glass high, to all who misstep,
To moments of laughter, like a joyful pep.
In the grand symphony, let chaos compose,
For joy is a tune that forever bestows.

Unraveled Threads of Humor

My sweater, unraveled, a scarf in disguise,
Each pull of the yarn showed my clumsy ties.
"Is it fashion?" they asked, with a curious grin,
I said, "Just a statement, let the fun begin!"

I mixed up my orders, for lunch at the mall,
A salad of jelly, with hotdogs on call.
The waiter just stood, caught between glee,
Said, "Best dish I've seen, just wait'll you see!"

I wore a big hat, a colorful mess,
Strangers all stared, at my daring excess.
But I strutted with pride, through the market I strolled,
Turns out every laugh breaks a fashion mold.

In tangled confusions, we find our delight,
With laughter as fabric, we weave day and night.
So here's to the humor, in threads that we spin,
For in every misstep, the joy lies within.

Serendipity and Snafus

I forgot my own birthday, but how could I pout?
The cake that I made, turned out quite a rout.
With candles made of spaghetti, a feast for a king,
The guests couldn't help but join in and sing.

A friend's surprise party, I showed up too early,
Brought combs and confetti, felt kind of surly.
But the host laughed aloud, "Well, you saved the day!"
Turned the frown on my face into laughter at play.

I mixed up my keys, they're in someone else's bag,
Now I'm stranded at Starbucks, my mood a bit lagged.
But I told a few jokes, shared coffee with glee,
My snafus spun magic, oh the fun that we see!

So let's toast to chance, to flukes we embrace,
With humor our guide, we find our own place.
In every odd twist, a spark we ignite,
Serendipity dances, as long as we're light-hearted and bright.

Giggles in the Gaps

In the chaos of each day,
We trip on shoes we shed away.
With every tumble, we all cheer,
Oh, what a sight when clumsiness is near!

Silly selfies, faces askew,
A splash of juice, all over you!
We laugh until our sides do ache,
These joyful blunders, oh make no mistake!

Missteps turn to stories told,
In patterns quirky, graceful and bold.
With friends beside, we squeal and sway,
Finding giggles in our disarray.

So here's to blunders, big and small,
In every fumble, we're having a ball.
Together we'll embrace the freaky art,
Of finding joy in the funny parts!

Clumsy Joy

Oh, the joy of dropping things,
A cup, a phone, and then it sings.
We laugh aloud at all the spills,
These happy accidents bring us thrills.

A dance that ends with two left feet,
Spinning wildly, oh, what a feat!
With each misstep, laughter breaks,
As we glide through our own mistakes.

Side-splitting tales of paths we roam,
Stumbling into the laugh-filled home.
Each trip and fall just adds to the fun,
Where clumsiness shines and joy's never done.

So let's embrace that awkward sway,
For it's in these moments, we find our way.
Together we'll laugh, both hard and loud,
In this clumsy joy, we're forever proud!

The Humor of Hindsight

Looking back on times gone by,
We chuckle softly, oh me, oh my!
The blunders make a tapestry bright,
Of lessons learned, our hearts ignite.

A missed step here, a wink there too,
Each moment laughter stuck like glue.
In the mirror, we see the grace,
Of giggles shared in life's mad race.

When wisdom knocks and thoughts collide,
We find the joy where thoughts reside.
With every slip, we find the fun,
Oh, the humor when all's said and done!

So raise a glass to memories sweet,
To every blip that made us complete.
In the rearview, we see it clear,
The gift of laughter we hold dear!

Fumbles and Flukes

In every fumble, a laugh awaits,
A shoe untied, the open gates.
We celebrate the silly turns,
For through each fluke, our spirit burns.

A coffee spill on Sunday morn,
An awkward laugh that leaves us torn.
Embracing quirks with open arms,
Each blunder adds to our many charms.

We stumble through our daily grind,
In these missteps, joy we find.
A wink, a grin, the lightness flows,
In every fumble, love only grows.

So here's to the laughs, the smiles we keep,
In moments clumsy, oh don't lose sleep!
For in this dance of flukes we prance,
We learn to laugh, and take our chance!

The Joke of Missed Opportunities

I slipped on an orange peel, so slick,
My grand exit turned into a comedy flick.
I waved at a stranger, thought it was a friend,
They blinked in confusion, oh where do I end?

A coffee spill lands like a Jackson Pollock,
My shirt looks like art, vibrant as a rock.
I texted the wrong group with a silly meme,
Now everyone's laughing, it's a shared dream.

I tripped on my shoelace, what a wild ride,
Fell into a puddle and giggled with pride.
A donut on my face, I wore it with flair,
Who knew sweet treats could fly through the air?

With quirky moments that come and they go,
I'll keep making memories, even in woe.
For every misstep, there's laughter to find,
A giggle, a chuckle, they're perfectly timed.

Laughter's Tapestry of Errors

I baked a cake, but the recipe lied,
It rose like a pancake, oh how I cried.
With sprinkles and frosting, it looked so divine,
A bite made me wonder, was it a bad sign?

Called an ex while tipsy, oh what a fun game,
Their voice on the line said, 'We're done, that's lame.'
I span in circles, how silly I seemed,
Staring at my phone, lost in a daydream.

An umbrella turned traitor in the spring breeze,
With every downpour, I laughed through the tease.
Drenched like a cat, but my heart was so light,
These blunders we share turn our frowns into flight.

In the gallery of goofs, I proudly display,
Memories of folly that brighten my day.
Let's weave our mistakes into laughter and cheer,
For nothing's more funny than friendship, my dear.

Comedic Crashes

I rode on my bike with great speed and delight,
But a squirrel crossed my path, oh what a fright!
I swerved to avoid, but fate had a joke,
Down went the bike, and up burst the smoke.

Tried cooking spaghetti, oh what a disaster,
The water boiled over, I was a real master.
Pasta flew everywhere, it danced like a pro,
In the middle of chaos, I began to glow.

A shopping cart raced with a mind of its own,
It veered to the right, my dignity flown.
As I crashed into shelves, all I could do,
Was laugh with the shoppers and bow in my shoe.

To stumble is human, so let's not regret,
Each mishap a puzzle we laugh to connect.
In the circus of errors, I'll juggle my way,
With humor and joy, come what may!

Blunders and Bubbles

I brought in a plant, thought green was my jam,
It turned a dull brown, but hey, I don't scram!
A cactus for company? What a good call!
At least it won't bother, no need for a small talk.

Went to a party, my shirt two sizes too tight,
I danced like a noodle, what a silly sight!
With laughter erupting, I twirled in a spin,
A blunder of fashion turned fun on a whim.

A bubble machine made for a scene out of dreams,
But I slipped on a bubble, it burst at the seams.
Rolling in laughter, my friends joined the spree,
Who knew that the slip might just set us free?

Through quirks and mistakes, we craft our own spins,
In this circus of life, let the giggles begin.
For blunders and bubbles are treasures so bright,
We'll toast to the chaos, grab a laugh and take flight.

The Quirks of What Went Wrong

I tripped on my shoelace, fell on my face,
Got up with a grin, in the silliest place.
A bird stole my sandwich, oh what a scene,
But laughter erupted, bright and serene.

I mixed up my notes, gave a speech on a cat,
While everyone snickered, imagine that!
With a wink and a nod, I rolled with the flow,
Mistakes keep us humble, isn't that so?

The cake that I baked, a disaster in sight,
It collapsed like my dreams on a Friday night.
But friends gathered 'round, they all had a slice,
And we laughed till we cried, oh isn't that nice?

In the dance of our blunders, we twirl and we sway,
Each misstep a step to a brighter display.
So here's to mistakes, with a chuckle and cheer,
For what's life without giggles, my dear?

Paints of Peculiar Paths

I painted a sky that turned green and pink,
With splatters of laughter, don't you think?
Every brush with a blunder, a stroke of delight,
Art's not perfect, but it's pure dynamite.

I tried to bake cookies, they came out as lumps,
A crunchy surprise that gave us the grumps.
But with every bite, giggles sprouted like seeds,
Peculiar paths grow into wondrous deeds.

I wore mismatched socks to a formal affair,
While folks tried to hold back their stifled air.
Every glance and chuckle sparked warmth in the room,
In folly we find how friendships can bloom.

In colors of chaos, we navigate fate,
Each quirky misstep, a reason to celebrate.
So let's dance with absurdity, sing out the refrain,
For paths less traveled can be cheerful and sane.

Revelations in Regret

I thought I could cook, burnt the toast to a crisp,
A puff of black smoke made us all laugh and lisp.
In the chaos of clatter, we found our delight,
Regrets are just tales that make wrongs feel right.

I sent a text meant for you to my boss,
A mix-up so funny, it felt like a loss.
But laughter erupted, tensions off-kilter,
Revelations in blunders teach us to filter.

I left my umbrella when caught in the rain,
Drenched to the bone, but I danced through the pain.
Each droplet a giggle, a splash of pure cheer,
Revelations in mishaps draw friends ever near.

Life's not a straight road, it's a zany parade,
With twists and with turns, and plans that degrade.
So here's to the laughter that lingers and spreads,
In moments of madness, we forge onward instead.

Jests in the Journey

I lost my way home in a maze made of maps,
With each turn I took, I just fell into traps.
But a stranger then laughed, showed me the bright way,
In jests of the journey, we're never led astray.

I wore two different shoes to an important meet,
Yet my charm turned the blunder into a feat.
With smiles all around, we shared stories galore,
In the dance of mistakes, we soar evermore.

I tripped on the pavement, stumbled and swayed,
While onlookers chuckled, unfazed and unfrayed.
The world's just a stage, with laughs as the cue,
In jests of the journey, let joy shine through.

So let's raise a glass to our accidental quests,
In every mishap, we uncover our best.
With laughter our compass, we'll wander and weave,
In the tapestry of folly, we learn how to believe.

Smiles Beneath the Stumbles

Tripped over my own two feet,
Laughter echoes down the street.
Banana peels, a common foe,
Yet here I am, putting on a show.

Each misstep leads to a grin,
Falling flat, but still, I win.
Dance through the blunders with flair,
What's a tumble when joy's in the air?

Mistakes are sprinkled like confetti,
Glimmering moments, calm and heady.
In goofy flops, the truth unfolds,
With every snicker, a tale retold.

So here's to stumbles, loud and clear,
In every fumble, I shed a tear.
Not of sadness, but pure delight,
For every fall brings laughter's light.

Hiccups and High Notes

Singing loud when the hiccups hit,
A melody born from a tiny split.
Off-key notes dance on the breeze,
Making music with effortless ease.

Plates may crash, but smiles arise,
Laughter spills like a sweet surprise.
Each awkward moment, a chance to join,
In the symphony of the not-so-fine.

With giggles wrapped in each refrain,
I'll serenade through joy and pain.
Savoring sweetness in every slip,
Letting the laughter spill from my lip.

So when the world tunes out of key,
Watch me shine, all wild and free.
Hiccups and high notes, a waltz we share,
In this funny dance, we find our flair.

Perfection in Imperfection

Like a painter with a crooked brush,
Creating art in a playful rush.
Splashed with colors inside the lines,
Finding beauty in the unconventional signs.

A jigsaw puzzle missing a piece,
A wacky smile that will never cease.
Oh, the chaos is sweetly unique,
A charming mess, it's all we seek.

Mistakes become our wildest muse,
In every blunder, joy to cruise.
Crafting laughter from simple flaws,
Breaking the rules with playful paws.

Join the dance of misfit dreams,
Where nothing is quite what it seems.
In the tapestry of errors spun,
We find that perfect is simply fun.

The Chaotic Comedies

A clown with shoes two sizes too big,
Strutting with flair, doing a jig.
Slips and slides across the floor,
With every tumble, joy galore.

Juggling tasks, a bowl of soup,
Spilling all while I try to swoop.
Giggles pop as I lose my grip,
Taking life on an oddball trip.

Pranks at play, the joy ignites,
In every chaos, laughter writes.
We stumble towards the next great scene,
With grins that glow and eyes that glean.

In this theater of the absurd,
Every misstep is blissfully blurred.
For in the chaos, we all agree,
The best kind of laughs set our spirits free.

Stumbles and Giggles

I tripped on my shoelace, oh what a sight,
Fell flat on my face, but the mood was light.
Laughter erupted, my friends held their breath,
As I bounced back up, defying my death.

A cake on the counter, I reached for a bite,
It slipped from my fingers and took a fast flight.
We laughed till we cried, in chocolate we rolled,
Memories were made as the stories were told.

The cat took a leap, missed the soft chair,
Came crashing down with a whirlwind of hair.
We couldn't stop chuckling at her fancy dive,
In every small mishap, we feel so alive.

With each clumsy moment, the joy multiplies,
We dance through the chaos, laughter our prize.
So here's to the stumbles, the giggles we share,
In this wild, funny world, we float like a pair.

The Art of Tripping Gracefully

With a wink and a smile, I stepped on a scene,
My foot found a puddle, it sparkled like green.
I flapped like a bird, arms outstretched in dismay,
My graceful performance had all gone astray.

I tried to impress, a dance on the floor,
But down came my heel, I could balance no more.
A pirouette ending with a tumble so grand,
The applause came from laughter, my fans couldn't stand.

In the kitchen I swayed, with sprouts in the air,
A flip and a slide, I was lost in the flair.
With veggies a-flying and giggles galore,
I became a salad, who could ask for more?

So here's to the limbs that flail and misstep,
To the art of the fall, and the laughter adept.
Embrace every tumble, each joking chance,
In this dance of misfortune, we twirl and we prance.

Echoes of Oops

I creaked through the door, thought I'd make a grand show,
But a slip on the mat led to quite the tableau.
With a tumble and roll, I found myself sprawled,
While echoes of laughter in the hallway enthralled.

A toast with my drink, I raised it up high,
A splash on my face made me question the sky.
From cheeks to the ceiling, the humor did soar,
So much for the quiet, what a ruckus we bore!

Knocking on wood could not save a few jokes,
Every sharp corner, a dance with some blokes.
We gathered 'round laughter, our friendship secured,
In echoes of oops, our hearts were assured.

So here's to the flubs that make memories bright,
To the giggles that come when things don't go right.
When life takes a turn, we lean in and say,
With each echo of oops, we find laughter's way.

Laughter Amidst the Blunders

In a game full of rules, I forgot all my moves,
I danced to my own beat, with no need to prove.
A wedgie, a stumble, oh what a parade,
Through laughter and snickers, our fun never fades.

Accidentally spilled, my drink on the floor,
I stood there and laughed, then I fell for it more.
With each slip and slide, we chortled and cheered,
As joy filled the room, the tension disappeared.

In our quest for perfection, we found a grand mess,
An oops and a giggle turned stress into zest.
With tales of misfortune, our spirits took flight,
In laughter's warm embrace, everything feels right.

So here's to the blunders that make our hearts sing,
To the joy in the chaos, and the smiles we bring.
When the world feels too rigid, let's break all the rules,
With laughter as ballast, we'll dance and be fools.

Melodies of Misfortune

Balloons in the air, a cake on the floor,
I tripped on my shoelace, but who's keeping score?
Twirling like a dancer, I spun with a grin,
It's laughter that wins when the chaos begins.

The dog stole my sandwich, I chased it around,
Laughter erupted, it echoed, it crowned.
With mustard and mayo, I'm wearing my snack,
But joy's in the moment, it never looks back.

Umbrellas flipped inside out in the storm,
We giggle and shuffle, oh how we conform!
With puddles and splashes, we dance on the street,
Messy as ever, but life's more than neat.

So gather the blunders, make notes of the falls,
Each stumble a rhythm, we answer the calls.
Put on a bright smile, the world is our stage,
Embracing our goofs as we turn the next page.

Chuckling Through the Cracks

Oh dear, I spilled coffee, what a sight to see,
The desk is a canvas, a wild jubilee.
My cat jumps in laughter, my desk it now claims,
We giggle together, no need for the shames.

I put on mismatched socks, it's a fashion faux pas,
But I strut with pride, I'm the weirdest of stars.
In crowded cafés, I wave and I smile,
Transforming my errors into humor and style.

The cooking disaster, the burnt toast we munch,
We laugh at the oven, behold this great lunch!
With a sprinkle of joy and a pinch of delight,
The best recipe comes with giggles in sight.

So here's to the fumbles, we celebrate loud,
In the chaos of being, we revel, we're proud.
For each little blunder adds sparkle to days,
A chuckle, a wink, in so many ways.

The Beauty of Blushing

I said the wrong name—it was such a big blunder,
Turns out, quite the joke; it put me asunder.
Blushing and laughing, my cheeks turn to fire,
With each awkward moment, I rise ever higher.

A joke told too loud in the middle of class,
The giggles erupt; the teacher won't pass!
But in all of the chaos, we cherish the joy,
The mishaps that come, far more fun to enjoy.

A friend dropped the microphone, oh what a scene,
With echoes of laughter, they turned ever green.
Yet the spirit of fun is a treasure we hold,
In blushes and giggles, pure happiness unfolds.

So flip those mistakes and embrace every cue,
For hiding in shadows means missing the view.
With laughter our chorus, we elevate the strife,
It's the beauty of moments that colors our life.

Smiles Between the Stumbles

I danced like a swan, but tripped on my feet,
Laughter erupted, oh, isn't that sweet?
With each little tumble, my heart starts to soar,
Finding joy in the chaos, who could ask for more?

A pie on my face was a birthday surprise,
Candles a-light, what a sight for the eyes!
With friends all around, the laughter spills out,
A recipe for joy, without any doubt.

Misplacing my keys, I'm searching for ages,
While friends roll in laughter, turning life's pages.
A moment of chaos is pure comedy's spark,
Each fold and each wrinkle, a bright little mark.

So grab hold of laughter, embrace every fall,
With imperfect grace, we'll have the best ball.
For every small stumble adds flair to our dance,
With smiles between stumbles, we find our romance.

Sparks of Spontaneity

One swift decision, a taco truck,
Turned into a dance with fate, oh what luck!
Spilled my drink, but who needs a seat?
Laughter echoes, life's spicy treat.

A fumble on my skateboard, what a show,
Hit a bump, went flying like a pro.
Clouds of giggles, friends roll on the floor,
Such blunders invite us to ask for more.

An unexpected road trip, we got lost,
But coffee stopped us from counting the cost.
With blaring laughter, the GPS went mad,
Each wrong turn turned a moment so glad.

We trip on our words, can't find the rhyme,
Yet every misstep is pure comedic time.
In every shortcoming, blooms a shared delight,
These sparks of folly ignite our bright night.

Tangle of Trials

I tried to bake a cake, oh what a mess,
Flour explosions leave me in distress.
The dog now wears frosting, a hat full of cheer,
But one glance at chaos, I couldn't help but sneer.

Lost my keys in the fridge, must be a sign,
Yesterday's spaghetti tangled like a vine.
Yet giggles bubble up, through all the fuss,
Every mix-up's a joke, riding the bus.

In yoga class, I misjudged my bend,
A graceful fall that brings a new trend.
Laughter erupts, my balance decided to snooze,
Every pose a reminder, we play and we lose.

Stumbling through trips, a life full of quirks,
Each fumble a treasure, we smirk as it lurks.
In this tangle of trials, let's savor each fall,
For laughter is brighter when we give it our all.

The Humor in Heartaches

Thought I found love under the moon's sweet glow,
Turns out he couldn't even tie his shoelaces, whoa!
A date gone wrong, but I laughed through the pain,
With each silly story, I'd do it again.

Saw my ex at the store, tripped on my feet,
Fell in the produce, a tumble so sweet.
Ripe avocado, they rolled at my side,
Yet humor blooms where our hearts tried to hide.

In the antics of heartache, there's always a twist,
Dancing in puddles made me feel blissed.
From clumsy rejections and mismatched attire,
Every tear spilled is less painful, but higher.

As we navigate messes, embrace them with glee,
For within every heartache, there's comedy.
In the laughter that follows, we find our new start,
A whimsical journey where joy plays its part.

Smirk at the Slip-ups

Stepped out in slippers, meant to wear shoes,
This fashion faux pas gives me giggles and soothes.
With a grin on my face, I stroll down the street,
Celebrating choices that can't be discreet.

When I mixed up the bus routes, oh what a ride,
Left my stop behind, with nowhere to hide.
But on this crazy journey, I found new friends,
Each laugh we shared, on adventure it bends.

Dropped my phone in the soup, it made quite the splash,
Said goodbye to my pictures, just a memory flash.
Yet every mishap brings a story to share,
In the soup of laughter, I thrive without care.

So let's toast to the times we wobbled and tripped,
With our hearts in the clouds, we've all been equipped.
Celebrate slip-ups, they lead us to play,
With smiles in the mix, seize the funny day!

The Pleasant Predicament

Fell down the stairs with a skip and a slide,
Laughed so hard, I forgot my pride.
Tripped on my shoelace in front of a crowd,
They burst into laughter, and I felt so proud.

Coffee in hand, I leaped up to cheer,
Spilled half of it, oh dear, oh dear!
Yet with each splash, a giggle did rise,
Who knew such joy could come in surprise?

Lost my way on a road full of bends,
Called up my buddy, who just made amends.
"Turn left here!" he said, "Or just go on straight!"
It's a mystery how I wound up so late!

All these moments, a clumsy ballet,
Swaying through life in a joyful display.
For every flop, there's a grin to be found,
In this comedy show, we're joyfully bound.

Witty Wreckage

Tried to impress with a fancy new dish,
Burnt it to ashes, but what's that? A wish!
Friends gathered round with forks in their hand,
Grilled cheese and laughter, just like we planned.

I set out to jog but just ended up strolling,
Found a dog's ball and started patrolling.
We raced down the street, both clumsy and wild,
No sweat on my brow, just a happy child.

A text to my crush went to Mom instead,
She laughed and replied, "That's a bold thread!"
What could've been awkward turned perfectly sweet,
A family dinner with unplanned retreat.

In this wreck where we tumble and spin,
Each mishaps a treasure, a cheeky grin.
For the messes we make are our stories to share,
With wit in the air and love everywhere!

The Bright Side of Blunders

Forgot my keys, locked out on the street,
Paced like a dancer, but oh how sweet!
Met a neighbor, with stories galore,
In our clumsy meeting, new friendships soar.

Burnt my dinner, smoke filled the room,
Called it a party, embraced the gloom.
With pizza in hand, we laughed till we cried,
What once was a mess now feels like pride.

Said the wrong name at a wedding toast,
But the bride just giggled, I raised a glass most.
Here's to the fumbles, the hiccups and slips,
To making more laughter and fun little trips!

In every misstep, there's joy to be found,
Life's little hiccups, hilariously profound.
So let's dance through the chaos, with grins ever wide,
And toast to the blunders that music our ride!

Echoes in the Unplanned

Forgot my umbrella, the sky opened wide,
Danced in the rain, feel that joyful tide.
Strangers all laughing, we splashed with delight,
In puddles we found a whimsical sight.

A picnic set up in the living room space,
Brought out the snacks, who cares about grace?
With blankets and stories piled high to the dome,
Our inside adventure felt just like home.

I stumbled on stage, my shoe went askew,
The audience cheered, so I bowed out too.
With laughter erupting, we made quite the scene,
In this charming chaos, I felt like a queen.

For every mistake that we sprinkle each day,
Echoes of laughter are never far away.
So here's to the moments not planned at all,
For they fill our days with the sweetest call.

Tripping Through the Tapestry

I stumbled on a pebble, oh what a sight,
My shoe took a left, while my heart took a flight.
With giggles from strangers, I bow and I grin,
Each fall turns to laughter, a dance I begin.

The coffee I spilled, a splash on my coat,
Yet somehow, my clumsiness got me a vote.
For best at mishaps, the crowd gave a cheer,
A toast with my cup, to all I hold dear.

A cake on my face, now that's quite the treat,
With friends bursting out, and no one can beat.
The joy in my folly, a jester's delight,
In blunders we find, the humor is bright.

So here's to my trips and blunders unplanned,
With each little slip, I take a firm stand.
For laughter's the magic, that we all should embrace,
In the tapestry woven, I'll find my own place.

Fortune in Fumbles

I dropped my phone, it flew like a bird,
Landed in pudding, oh what a absurd.
Riches in giggles, I'll take that instead,
For fortune in fumbles, my laughter is fed.

A sandwich went flying, a cat caught my lunch,
The chaos around me, a glorious punch.
With crumbs on my chin, I wave my white flag,
In this game of blunders, I'm never a drag.

The first date I flopped, misread every sign,
Tripped over my heart, but still felt divine.
For every mistake, a story to share,
With humor and folly, I walk without care.

So raise up your glass to the blunders we make,
In laughter we find, it's more than a shake.
The fortune in fumbles, the gold that we hold,
Is the joy of our journeys, more precious than gold.

Reflections on the Road Less Taken

I took the wrong road, the map was a joke,
Found donuts in laughter, where I thought I'd choke.
For every wrong turn, a treat on the way,
With smiles and with giggles, I'm here to stay.

A traffic jam dance, the cars bumping along,
With snacks in my lap, I just sing my song.
The honks turn to music, as friends join the show,
In chaos and joy, our laughter will grow.

I missed my exit, oh what a surprise!
But stumbled on wonders, right under the skies.
Each twist and each turn, a tale to unfold,
With chuckles and cheer, my heart stays bold.

So here's to the paths, that twist and that twine,
For every weird journey, I call it divine.
The road less taken, is where we find cheer,
With laughter as compass, we'll wander without fear.

Laughter Echoes in Flaws

Oh, the soup that I spilled, it splashed in a dance,
With noodles like ribbons, I took a bold chance.
The chaos surrounding, a whirlwind of fun,
In laughter's embrace, my worries are done.

I wore mismatched socks, a color parade,
With friends all around, my quirks never fade.
For every odd choice, a giggle to share,
In a world that's perfect, I simply don't care.

Each trip and each fall, a comic refrain,
With humor as sunshine, I welcome the rain.
These echoes of laughter, like music will play,
In the symphony crafted, we find our own way.

So let's toast to the flops, the mishaps, and more,
To the moments of silver, we can't help but adore.
For in the grand mess, it's the joy we embrace,
In laughter's sweet echo, we all find our place.

www.ingramcontent.com/pod-product-compliance
Lightning Source LLC
Chambersburg PA
CBHW051650160426
43209CB00004B/858